庭 GARDEN VIEWS III
WATER & STREAM GARDENS

TATSUI TEIEN KENKYUJO

Contents / 目 次

Color Plates／カラー図版 ——————————————————— 3

Explanation by Takenosuke Tatsui／日本の庭の水（龍居竹之介）——— 97

Plan／庭の図面 ———————————————————————— 117

List／作庭家リスト ————————————————————— 124

Map／日本地図 ——————————————————————— 126

Afterword／あとがき ———————————————————— 127

Photographs / Osamu Nobuhara（信原 修）
English / Shigemaru Shimoyama（下山重丸）
Book design / Eikō Iwakuro（岩黒永興）

1 Yokoi Estate : Iwate (Work of Kyōichi Chiba)〜 *Garden stream with the colorful flowers.*
横井邸：岩手（千葉恭一作品）〜草花がいろどりを添える流れの姿

2 Yokoi Estate : Iwate (Work of Kyōichi Chiba)～ *Depth is given to this garden by the planting work, in which a Rankei-style stone lantern was placed.*
　横井邸：岩手（千葉恭一作品）〜植栽で厚みを出し蘭渓形燈籠を添える

3 Kanno Estate：Iwate (Work of Hiroshi Moniwa)〜 *Garden stream expressing the pleasant feeling of nature.*
管野邸：岩手（茂庭弘作品）〜自然な感じをよくあらわした流れ

4　Kikuchi Estate：Iwate (Work of Hiroshi Moniwa)〜 *The garden pond in peaceful atmosphere.　The path using large flagstones controls the scene.*
　　菊地邸：岩手（茂庭弘作品）〜穏やかなたたずまいの池。大きな敷石園路が景を締める

5 Ōba Estate : Fukushima (Work of Asaji Moroi)～ *For this garden stream the variety of movements of water is given by a number of small drops in elevation.*
大場邸：福島（諸井浅次作品）～小さな段差で水の動きに変化をつけた流れ

6   Kobata Estate : Fukushima (Work of Michio Moroi)～ *The naturalistic shore work of the garden stream and the water flowing among the straight-line work of the stone pavement.*
木幡邸：福島(諸井道雄作品)～自然風護岸と直線構成の敷石の中を行く流れ

7 Uzu Estate : Tochigi (Work of Kōji Ikeda)～ *The plank bridge matches with the rustic stream scene.*
宇津邸：栃木(池田幸司作品)～木の橋もひなびた流れにはよく似合う

8 Uzu Estate : Tochigi (Work of Kōji Ikeda) ~ *The shore work of this pond represents some scenes we notice in the natural stream.*
宇津邸：栃木（池田幸司作品）〜自然の渓流に見られる景色を護岸に写した池

9 Nihira Estate : Tochigi (Work of Toshiki Takamatsu) ～ *The scene looks as through a mountain side spring water is running down.*
仁平邸：栃木（高松俊樹作品）～山からの湧き水が流れ落ちる姿を再現するかのようだ

10 Nihira Estate：Tochigi (Work of Toshiki Takamatsu)〜 *The stone bridge controls the view and gives depth the whole scene.*
仁平邸：栃木（高松俊樹作品）〜石橋で眺めを引き締めて池に奥行きを出す

11 N Estate：Saitama (Work of Kōji Matsumoto)〜 *The water from the bamboo piping becomes the stream by way of the basin.*
N邸：埼玉（松本孔志作品）〜筧からの水は手水鉢伝いに流れとなる

12 Saitō Estate：Saitama (Work of Seigaku Nakamura)〜 *The layout around Tsukubai basin makes an elegant view.*
斉藤邸：埼玉(中村青岳作品)〜格調ある姿を形づくる蹲踞まわりの景

13 Itō Estate : Saitama (Work of Seigaku Nakamura)～ *The Tsukubai basin near the veranda head emits a pleasant sound of water from Kakehi, the bamboo pipe.*
伊藤邸：埼玉(中村青岳作品)～縁先近くの蹲踞は筧遣いの水音が快い

14 Nagoya Estate：Tokyo (Work of Eiichi Kawayauchi)～ *A square water bowl in placed in the stone-paved terrace of straight-line design.*
名古屋邸：東京(川谷内映一作品)～直線構成の石敷きテラスに正方形の水鉢を添える

15 Daitō Gakuen : Tokyo (Work of Eiichi Kawayauchi)〜 *The interior garden of Tsukubai, where the diagonal line of Nobedan path makes the main feature.*
大東学園:東京(川谷内映一作品)〜斜めに走る延段でアクセントをつけた蹲踞の中庭

16 Itō Estate：Tokyo (Work of Ken Dōke)～ *The garden stream runs through a beautiful stone setting.*
伊藤邸：東京（道家健作品）～美しい石組の間を縫って流れがつくられる

17　Itō Estate：Tokyo (Work of Ken Dōke)〜 *The garden of stone arrangement and stream as viewed from the residence interior.*
伊藤邸：東京(道家健作品)〜室内から石組と流れを持つ庭を眺める

18 Uematsu Estate : Tokyo (Work of Toshiyuki Iwasawa)～ *The shore view of this pond was given a variety by using smallish cobbles.*
　　植松邸：東京(岩沢俊之作品)～小ぶりの石で汀の姿に変化をつけた池

19 Muraki Estate：Tokyo (Work of Ken Dōke)〜 *The garden stream quietly running at the side of Nobedan path appears nature itself.*
村木邸：東京（道家健作品）〜延段園路の脇を静かに進む流れは自然そのものだ

20 Kuze Estate：Tokyo (Work of Sozan Kawamura)〜 *An orthodox Tsukubai setting and its surroundings.*
　　久世邸：東京(河村素山作品)〜オーソドックスな構えの蹲踞まわりの眺め

21 Shiga Estate : Tokyo (Work of Chiaki Kobayashi) ~ *The garden of Tsukubai and stream as viewed from inside the room.*
志賀邸:東京(小林千秋作品)〜室内から見た蹲踞と流れを持つ庭

22 Kashima Estate : Tokyo (Work of Eiichi Kawayauchi) ~ *The roof garden with a Tsukubai basin.*
鹿島邸：東京(川谷内映一作品)～2階屋上につくられた蹲踞のある庭

23　Kashima Estate：Tokyo (Work of Eiichi Kawayauchi)〜 *Around the Tsukubai basin set at the central far end of No.22.*
鹿島邸：東京(川谷内映一作品)〜22の中央奥に組まれた蹲踞まわり

24　Itabashi Estate：Tokyo (Work of Toshiyuki Iwasawa)〜 *The pond designed in the arc and straight line can be softened by using some pebbles.*
板橋邸：東京(岩沢俊之作品)〜弧と直線で構成した池は小石の扱いで柔らか味がある

25　Itabashi Estate : Tokyo (Work of Toshiyuki Iwasawa) ~ *The garden stream using for its source a water bowl designed by the gardener himself.*
板橋邸：東京（岩沢俊之作品）〜作者デザインの水鉢を水源とした流れ

26 Meikō Shōkai：Tokyo (Work of Ken Dōke)〜 *This dynamic stone arrangement utilizes the objet d'art water basin for its attraction center.*
明光商会：東京(道家健作品)〜石造品利用の手水鉢を中心にした迫力ある石組

27   Niigaki Estate : Tokyo (Work of Takeyuki Itakura)〜 *A certain brightness is noticed on the water basin set among the low, thick planting work.*
　　新垣邸：東京(板倉武幸作品)〜低く密植した中に据えた手水鉢には明るさもある

28   Ōki Estate : Tokyo (Work of Sozan Kawamura)〜 *The view of Tsukubai and its surrounding as seen from the house interior is also attractive.*
大木邸：東京（河村素山作品）〜室内から眺めた蹲踞まわりは景としても美しい

29　Ōhara Estate：Tokyo (Work of Miki Fujino)～ *The area of the water basin is well brightened by the sand spreading.*
大原邸：東京(藤野三樹作品)～敷砂で明るさもよく出た手水鉢まわりのようす

30 Yamaguchi Estate : Tokyo (Work of Toshio Hashimoto) ~ *The straight line of Nobedan path and the Yukimi-style stone lantern are making the pond shore view effective.*
山口邸：東京（橋本年男作品）～直線の延段と雪見形石燈籠で池畔を締めた池

31 D Building Roof Garden : Tokyo (Work of Chiaki Kobayashi)～ *The stone well-curb plays the source of the garden stream.*
大東京火災海上保険：東京(小林千秋作品)～流れの水源には石を組んだ井筒(井戸)をあてている

32 Naitō Estate : Tokyo (Work of Takayuki Hirai) ~ *Garden with the Tsukubai in center as viewed from inside the room.*
内藤邸：東京（平井孝幸作品）〜室内から眺めた蹲踞を中心にまとめた庭

33 Nakamura Estate : Tokyo (Work of Tōkai Zōen)～ *Looking from the room interior the garden built in the second floor with Tsukubai basin as its main feature.*
中村邸：東京（東海造園作品）～2階につくられた蹲踞主体の庭を室内から眺める

34 Usami Estate：Tokyo (Work of Yamamoto Zōen)〜 *Water from the stone basin helps creating a hillside village air.*
宇佐美邸：東京(山本造園作品)〜山里のムードを出すのに手水鉢の水も力を貸している

35 Imaeda Estate : Tokyo (Work of Tōkai Zōen)〜 *Water from the stone basin controlled the view of inner approach.*
今枝邸：東京（東海造園作品）〜室内のアプローチの景は手水鉢の水が締める

36 Sasa Estate：Tokyo (Work of Mitsukoshi Dept.)～ *Water of the Tsukubai plays the key point also for the second floor veranda garden.*
佐々邸：東京(三越作品)～2階ベランダの庭も蹲踞の水がポイント

37 Sasa Estate：Tokyo (Work of Mitsukoshi Dept.)〜 *Looking from the side of Tsukubai in No.36, showing the narrowness of the space.*
佐々邸：東京(三越作品)〜36の蹲踞を横から見ると狭いことがわかる

38 N Estate：Tokyo (Work of Azabu Ueyū)〜 *The stream was constructed using the narrow space of the room interior.*
N邸：東京(麻布 植祐作品)〜室内のわずかなスペースにつくった流れ

39 N Estate : Tokyo (Work of Azabu Ueyū) ~ *Ichimonji-style water basin is giving a Japanese air in the porch.*
N邸：東京(麻布 植祐作品)～一文字形の手水鉢が玄関に趣を出すこととなっている

40 Tsukiji Uemura Takanawa Saryō : Tokyo (Work of Hayama Zōen) ～ *Tsukubai setting in the corner of this house goes well with the flower on the wall.*
つきじ植むら 高輪茶寮：東京（羽山造園作品）～室内の一角に設けた蹲踞は壁面の花生けともよく合う

41　Hotel Tokyo：Tokyo (Work of Azabu Ueyū)～ *The pattern on the Ginkakuji-style water basin somehow matches with the rhombus of the bamboo fence.*
ホテル東京：東京(麻布 植祐作品)～銀閣寺形の手水鉢の模様と竹垣の菱がマッチして面白い

42　Hyōtanya：Tokyo (Work of Tōkai Nōen)～ *Interior garden where the bold arrangement of the water wheel is shown.*
　　ひょうたんや：東京（東海農園作品）〜大胆に水車を扱った室内の庭

43 Hyōtanya : Tokyo (Work of Tōkai Nōen)～ *The water wheel in No.42 is the point view at the far ènd of the entrance.*
ひょうたんや：東京（東海農園作品）〜42の水車は入口奥の眺めのポイントである

44 Serina：Tokyo (Work of Seiwa Zōen)〜 *The waterfall built on the third floor looks quite natural.*
瀬里奈：東京(成和造園作品)〜3階フロアにつくられた瀧には自然の味がある

45 Budōya : Tokyo (Work of Seiji Imanaka) ～ *The cascade built at a corner of the second floor reaches upward to the fourth floor.*
葡萄屋：東京(今中征治作品)～2階の一隅につくられた瀧は吹抜け構造のため4階に達する

46 Amano Estate : Kanagawa (Work of Tomio Inoue)～ *Viewing the stream flowing delicately to right and left.*
　　天野邸：神奈川（井上富雄作品）～微妙に左右する流れのようすを見る

47 Amano Estate : Kanagawa (Work of Tomio Inoue)〜 *The scene of waterfall and stream built by using the previously existed stones.*
天野邸：神奈川（井上富雄作品）〜以前からあった石を利用してつくった瀧と流れのようす

48 Kawada Estate : Kanagawa (Work of Toshio Hashimoto)～ *The garden stream flows through and over the rocks.*
川田邸：神奈川(橋本年男作品)～石を伝い石をわけて進む流れの風情

49   Nakamura Estate : Kanagawa (Work of Mikio Tomita)〜 *The bird bath made in the sense of a wash basin plays the key point of the garden.*
中村邸：神奈川(富田幹雄作品)〜手水鉢の感じにつくられたバードバスは庭のポイントとなる

50 Itoga Estate : Kanagawa (Work of Hiroshi Nakamura) ~ *The scene gives the air of a real stream in nature.*
    糸賀邸：神奈川(中村寛作品)〜沢の風情を示すかのような流れのようす

51   Itoga Estate : Kanagawa (Work of Hiroshi Nakamura)～ *The entire scene around the water basin of No.50 is a successful work representing nature.*
　　　糸賀邸：神奈川（中村寛作品）～50の手水鉢まわりの全景で自然そのもの

52 Abe Estate : Kanagawa (Work of Masayuki Kojima)～ *The source of water running down from the water basin shows a variety of lovely expressions in its course.*
阿部邸：神奈川（小嶋正行作品）～水源となる手水鉢からの水は流れに落ちて豊かな表情を見せる

53 Suzuki Estate : Kanagawa (Work of Masayuki Kojima) ~ *This arrangement of the water basin and stream gives a well settled mood.*
鈴木邸：神奈川（小嶋正行作品）～落ち着いたムードの手水鉢まわりと流れの姿

54 Kōmyōji Temple : Kanagawa (Work of Tomio Inoue)~ *This design of garden stream reminds us of a mountain stream in nature.*
光明寺:神奈川(井上富雄作品)~山間の谷川を思わせる流れのデザイン

55 Kōmyōji Temple : Kanagawa (Work of Tomio Inoue)~ *This stone bowl of an interesting shape becomes the sourse of water for No.54.*
光明寺：神奈川（井上富雄作品）～54の水源となる石の鉢は形そのものがおもしろい

56 SY Estate : Kanagawa (Work of Toshiyuki Iwasawa) ～ *The water running from the spring behind this garden becomes a stream after filling the pond in its course.*
ＳＹ邸：神奈川（岩沢俊之作品）～水は奥の水源から池を経て流れに進む

57　Tsuruoka Estate：Niigata (Work of Sōichirō Kinoshita)〜 *Tsukubai and the stream with the Oribe-style stone lantern in the background.*
鶴岡邸：新潟（木下荘一郎作品）〜織部形石燈籠を背にした蹲踞と流れのようす

58 Hirasawa Estate : Niigata (Work of Ikechū Zōen)～ *Waterfall constructed with a number of steps gives a variety of expressions to the dropping water.*
　　平澤邸：新潟（池忠造園作品）～何段にも構成した瀧は水の表情に変化を与える

59 Hirasawa Estate：Niigata (Work of Ikechū Zōen)～ *The pond has a thick stand of trees in background.*
　　平澤邸：新潟（池忠造園作品）～深い木立をバックにした池のたたずまい

60   Y Estate : Niigata (Work of Takao Donuma)～ *The water from the garden stream flows into the pond designed emphasizing straight lines.*
Y邸：新潟(土沼隆雄作品)〜流れからの水は直線を強調した池に注がれる

61　Y Estate：Niigata (Work of Wakasugi Zōen)〜 *The water from the highly set stone work drops into the pond below.*
　　Y邸：新潟（若杉造園作品）〜高く構えた瀧石組からの水は下の池に落ちる

62 Terao Estate : Niigata (Work of Takeuchi Zōen)～ *The water starts at the far end of the garden and finally poures into the pond.*
　　寺尾邸：新潟(竹内造園作品)～水は奥から流れを経て池に注ぐ

63 Terao Estate : Niigata (Work of Takeuchi Zōen) ~ *When viewed from inside the house the pond gives the feeling of depth to the garden.*
　　寺尾邸：新潟（竹内造園作品）〜室内から眺めて奥深さを感じさせる池のようす

64 Sekikawa Estate : Niigata (Work of Takeuchi Zōen)～ *The scene of the water from the Tsukubai can be fully enjoyed from inside the house also.*
関川邸：新潟(竹内造園作品)～手水鉢からの水の景は室内からも十分に楽しめる

65 Ibe Estate : Niigata (Work of Matsutarō Kanda)～ *This water scene with bamboo piping gives the mood of a running spring in the mountain side.*
　　井部邸：新潟（神田松太郎作品）～山中の清水といったムードも備えた筧遣いの水景

66　Maruta Estate：Niigata (Work of Shōzō Ishikawa)～ *Tsukubai enclosed by the planting work presents a nonchalant view.*
　　丸田邸：新潟(石川昇造作品)～植栽に囲まれた蹲踞はさりげなく1つの景をなしている

67 Tomita Estate : Niigata (Work of Hokuriku Zōen) ～ *A waterscape composed of Mizubotaru-style stone lantern and a water basin.*
　　富田邸：新潟（北陸造園作品）～水蛍形石燈籠と手水鉢でまとめた水の景観

68 Takahashi Estate : Niigata (Work of Hokuriku Zōen)～ *Ori-Tsukubai or "step-down" Tsukubai basin set at far end of the garden gives a quiet air around.*
高橋邸：新潟(北陸造園作品)～奥まって低く組まれた降り蹲踞の周辺は静寂そのものだ

69 Tachibana Estate : Ishikawa (Work of Katsuyoshi Kishi)〜 *The shore of the stream is surrounded by bushes and wild grasses.*
立花邸：石川(城至勝義作品)〜低木と山野草で護岸を包んだ流れ

70 Arashi Estate：Ishikawa (Work of Tomio Takebayashi)～ *Garden stream with bold treatment of stones viewed from the house interior.*
嵐邸：石川（竹林臣夫作品）～豪快な石遣いの流れのようすを室内から眺める

71　Mukaide Estate : Ishikawa (Work of Takeshi Tachibana)～ *Tsukubai setting and Nobedan path give a modern mood.*
　　向出邸：石川（立花武志作品）～モダンなムードを感じさせる蹲踞石組と延段園路

72 Araki Estate：Ishikawa (Work of Takeshi Tachibana)〜 *Looking from house interior the Tsukubai basin which is the central scene of the garden.*
荒木邸：石川（立花武志作品）〜庭のポイントとなる蹲踞を室内から眺める

73 Okada Estate : Ishikawa (Work of Shigeji Takebayashi)～ *Conforming to the owner's request the stream and its water sourse were all designed in naturalistic manner.*

岡田邸：石川（竹林繁二作品）〜流れとその水源は自然風にというオーナー案に従った庭

74 Kimishita Estate：Ishikawa (Work of Shigeji Takebayashi)～ *Only one pine tree is seen in front. This is because of the consideration of the seasonal snow removing from the roof .*
公下邸：石川（竹林繁二作品）～手前にはマツしか見えないが、これは屋根の雪おろしを考慮しての植栽方法

75   Honda Estate：Ishikawa (Work of Tomigo Ichimura)〜 *The reason of not feeling the thick planting is because of the pruning technique used to avoid the snow piling.*
本田邸：石川（市村冨五作品）〜あまり樹木の厚味を感じないのは、雪が積もらない剪定方法をとっているためだ

76 Hayashi Estate：Ishikawa (Work of Seikichi Matsumoto)～ *The garden has a peaceful atmosphere by a single Indian Lilac. However, in winter the snow covers all over there.*
林邸：石川（松本清吉作品）〜１本のサルスベリによって穏やかに見える景も、冬場は雪の壁と化してしまうそうだ

77 Hanamurasaki：Ishikawa (Work of Kōzō Iwatani)～ *For the approach to the main bath hall a pleasant water scene is built also.*
花紫：石川（岩谷浩三作品）～大浴場への通路にも水景がつくられて目を楽しませる

78 Hanamurasaki : Ishikawa (Work of Kōzō Iwatani)~ *Lobby garden in which the character of the material is shown by the modernistic treatment.*
花紫：石川（岩谷浩三作品）～素材の個性を生かし現代的にアレンジしたロビーの庭

79 Hanamurasaki : Ishikawa (Work of Kōzō Iwatani)~ *Front view of No.78 small garden composed of two water basins with the pile of Kiso-ishi riverstones in background.*
花紫：石川（岩谷浩三作品）～78の木曽石の石積を背景に水鉢2つを扱った小庭を正面から見る

80 Hotel Rantei : Kyoto (Work of Saburō Sone)~ *Arrangement of the original type water basin and its surroundings.*
ホテル嵐亭：京都（曽根三郎作品）～創作の手水鉢とその周辺の構成

81 Hotel Rantei : Kyoto (Work of Saburō Sone)～ *A skillful combination of the hexagonal stone paving and the water basin.*
ホテル嵐亭：京都（曽根三郎作品）～六角形の亀甲張りの敷石を巧みに手水鉢と組み合わす

82 Maruoka Estate : Kyoto (Work of Takahiro Inoue)～ *The bold treatment of rocks forming the stream of water.*
丸岡邸：京都（井上剛宏作品）～大胆な石の組み合わせで水の流れを形づくっている

83　Maruoka Estate：Kyoto (Work of Takahiro Inoue)〜 *The rich expression of the water surface is quite attractive.*
丸岡邸：京都（井上剛宏作品）〜水面の表情の豊かさには目を見張らされる

84 Nakanishi Estate : Kyoto (Work of Kōzō Okamoto)～ *View of the stepping stones and water basin laid in the forecourt.*
中西邸：京都(岡本耕蔵作品)～前庭に打たれた飛石と手水鉢の眺め

85 Mori Estate : Kyoto (Work of Shōji Inohana)～ *The well-curb setting behind is also contributing to the garden scene.*
森邸：京都(猪鼻昌司作品)～奥の井筒も水景を表現する材料の1つ

86 Mori Estate : Kyoto (Work of Shōji Inohana)～ *The Tsukubai basin and its surroundings.*
森邸：京都(猪鼻昌司作品)～蹲踞とその周辺のようす

87   Myōdōji Temple：Kyoto (Work of Minoru Fujii)～ *A unique Tsukubai making use of a bridge-post stone for the water bowl.*
　　　明道寺：京都(藤井稔作品)～橋脚石を水鉢とした個性的な蹲踞

88 Reimei Church Seminary：Kyoto (Work of Hideo Tsuda)～ *The forecourt is finished with treatment of the stone gutter.*
 黎明教会研修所：京都(津田秀夫作品)～前庭は石樋をあしらったものに仕上げている

89 Reimei Church Seminary : Kyoto (Work of Hideo Tsuda) ~ *Water basin showing the designer's creativity.*
　　黎明教会研修所：京都（津田秀夫作品）〜個性的な趣を伝える創作の手水鉢

90 Higuchi Estate：Kyoto (Work of Yasuo Kitayama)〜 *Water basin set in the far end of garden.*
樋口邸：京都（北山安夫作品）〜庭の最奥部にある手水鉢のようす

91 Takuma Estate : Kyoto (Work of Masafumi Kobayashi)~ *The erect type water basin controlling the court garden by its simple design.*
宅間邸：京都(小林正典作品)～シンプルな構成を示す中庭を締める立手水鉢

92 Kamii Estate : Kyoto (Work of Yukio Terasaki)～ *Court garden giving a settled air contributes to this waterscape.*
神居邸：京都（寺崎幸雄作品）〜落ち着いた雰囲気を出す坪庭も水景を描きあげる

93 Ueda Estate : Nara (Work of Shōji Inohana) ~ *The main garden has waterfall and stream of the dry landscape style.*
上田邸：奈良（猪鼻昌司作品）～枯瀧と枯流れを持つ主庭

94　Ueda Estate：Nara (Work of Shōji Inohana)～ *The waterscape was extended by way of the long flumes (bamboo piping).*
　　上田邸：奈良（猪鼻昌司作品）～長い筧で水の景の延長をはかる

STREAM GARDEN by Moronobu Hishikawa＝Ukiyoe printer, 17C＝
17世紀に浮世絵師・菱川師宣が描いた流れの庭（『餘景作り庭の図』から）

EXPLANATION —— TAKENOSUKE TATSUI

1　The Pond (1) (2)

2　Nagare, the Stream (1) (2) (3) (4)

3　The Tsukubai (1) (2) (3)

4　The Chozubachi (1) (2)

5　The Waterfall

6　Izutsu and Bridges

7　Kakehi and Suisha

解　説 ——— 龍居竹之介

1　池(1) (2)

2　流れ(1) (2) (3) (4)

3　蹲踞(1) (2) (3)

4　手水鉢(1) (2)

5　瀧

6　井筒と橋

7　筧と水車

1 The Pond (1)

The pond in the Japanese garden usually takes the form of some pond in nature reproduced in reduced scale. Consequently the constructed pond mostly shows its complicated shore lines.

When the planting work is added to it, the shore line is hidden here and there and gives the depth to the scenery reminding us that of nature.

1 池 (1)

日本の庭の池は、おおむね自然の縮小という形をとっている。従ってその形は曲線が多く、入り組んだ汀線を持ったものがよく見られる。

それに植栽を施すと護岸の部分が見え隠れするとともに、奥行きも深くなってますます自然の景観を偲ばすものとなる。

2

63

75

59

83

POND & BRIDGE = by old gardening book
(『石組園生八重垣伝』より)

30

4

18

8

93

1 The Pond (2)

Many of the ponds in the Japanese garden recently designed have works of modern formative art while keeping empasis on the nature's way as before. A good example is the use of cut stones in order to bring about the mood of straight lines.

Associating with modern architecture, the pond can be built on the top of building as well as inside the room. There is a new idea and practice of the modernization of the early Japanese style of pond also.

1 池 (2)

現代の日本の庭の池の中には、かつての自然重視というデザインのほかに、造形的なデザインを試みるものも多くなっている。加工石を用いて直線を主体としたものもその一例である。

現代建築の屋上、室内にもつくられることの多くなった現代では、特に古典的な日本式の池の現代化が目立ってきてもいる。

24

22

60

79

78

2 Nagare, the Stream (1)

Nagare, or the stream is one of the gardening techniques of handling water. The running stream in the garden is highly appreciated since it brings into the garden the feeling of the valley and brook scene of nature as well as giving the pleasant sound of water.

Recently we see such examples as the combination of the artificial cut stones and the scene of flowing water. They show the concern of the modern aspect of the garden designers in Japan.

2 流 れ (1)

庭の中での水の扱いの一つに、流れという手法がある。渓谷、小川のような風景を庭の中につくり出す感じのこの流れは、水の動きと音の楽しみも人にもたらせるため、大変喜ばれる。

加工した石とごく自然な感じを出した流れという組み合わせも最近は見られ、ここにも現代の日本の庭の工夫が覗かれる。

52

73

62

53

6

2 Nagare, the Stream (2)

Among the garden stream designs are examples which try to show the source of water openly, instead of the traditional method of concealing it from direct view. The purpose of the revealing method is to make the water source the main point of attraction.

For the latter purpose the *Chozubachi* style of water basin is mostly used. Water is first contained there, from which water may gush out and dropped into the stream.

2 流れ (2)

庭の中の流れには、水源をはっきり見せようとするデザインのものも少なくない。水源をつくることによってこれも庭の一つのポイントになるという利点があるせいでもある。

水源とし用いられるものの大半は手水鉢式のものである。ここに一旦、水を溜め、または噴き出させて流れに落とすわけだ。

64

21

57

13

11

STREAM

67

65

55

49

25

2 Nagare, the Stream (3)

How to control the motion of the water is an interesting part of the design. Since the purpose of making the stream in the Japanese garden is to bring about a scene in nature, the stream shore is built with natural rocks and wild plants are provided there.

The stream course itself is given some complicated small turns so that it flows down turning to right and left.

2 流 れ (3)

流れのデザインの面白さは水の動きをどうコントロールするかにある。日本の庭では流れも山野の水の景色を写そうとするために、自然石で岸辺を組んで、そこに山野の草花を植えることになる。

そして流れ自体も複雑な小曲がりをつけて、水を右に左に向きを変えながら落としていく形が一般的といえる。

1

3

82

9

5

"YATSUHASHI" BRIDGE & POND

54

56

69

48

46

2 Nagare, the Stream (4)

Waterfalls are usually built at the remote side of the garden, but in the case of the garden stream, in order to show the motion of water more effectively, it is often built close to the building.

The designing of stream for indoors or close to the house is not easy since it becomes the central view of the garden not to mention the careful study of the motion of water.

2 流 れ (4)

瀧などは庭の奥につくることが多いが、流れの場合は建物近くにつくることも少なくない。むしろ建物近くに水源を持った流れのほうが水の動きがよく見えると喜ばれることもある。

室内、あるいは部屋のすぐ外につくる流れは水の動きもさることながら、庭の主景となるためデザインはさらに難しいといえる。

70

16

19

38

17

3 The Tsukubai (1)

The Tsukubai is bacically an equipment for washing hands and rinsing mouth before the guest enter the room where to enjoy tea ceremony. The main part of the Tsukubai setting is the water basin (called *Mizubachi*) with brimming clear water. Then two stones are placed in right and left front of the *Mizubachi*. The one is for placing a hot water pail on it in winter, and another for placing the light such as candle on it.

Nowadays, however, Tsukubai is used more scenic purpose in the garden without reference to the tea ceremony.

3 蹲踞 (1)

蹲踞はもともと、茶の湯を楽しむ部屋〈茶室〉にはいる前に、口や手を清めるために備えた設備である。主体となるのは水をたたえた手水鉢（水鉢ともいう）。その左右に冬に湯を入れた桶を置く石と、照明用のロウソクなどの手明かりを置く石を据える。

現在では茶の湯と無関係に庭の景色として使うことがふえた。

66

72

20

12

84

3 The Tsukubai (2)

Usually a stone lantern is placed around Tsukubai. This is for the lighting Tsukubai when used at night. However, the two features should be considered as making a scenic set more than their original functions.

The stone lantern set around Tsukubai is usually footless burying style because its height can be adjusted easily.

3 蹲踞 (2)

蹲踞の周囲には普通、石燈籠を配置する。これは夜間、蹲踞を用いるときの照明用ということだが、むしろこれも蹲踞とセットの形で考えられていると考えたほうがよい。

蹲踞まわりの石燈籠は普通、下部を地中に埋め込む形式のものが多い。これは高さの調節ができるからでもある。

87

27

86

68

23

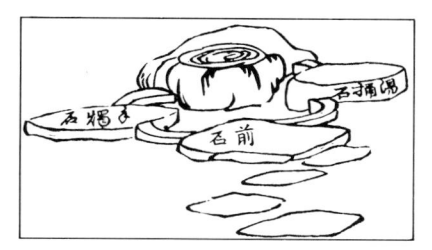

"TSUKUBAI" WATER BASIN

34

90

33

32

76

3 The Tsukubai (3)

Since Tsukubai, the low style of stone basin, can make an independent view by itself, it is used in the roof garden, indoors and others. In a place with insufficient depth a Tsukubai with a planting behind brings some Japanese mood easily.

In some interior court garden where the planing is difficult, the bold treatment of space may be possible by an effective design of the Tsukubai view.

3 蹲踞 (3)

蹲踞はそれだけで一つの形を生むために、屋上の庭、あるいは室内などでもよくつくられている。奥行きのない場所では背後に植え込みをつくると、それだけで、なんとなく日本式の庭のムードが出るものである。

また中庭などで植栽も不可能なときは、蹲踞中心のデザインを生かして、大胆な空間処理も果たすことができる。

36

35

37

15

28

4   The Chozubachi (1)

Chozubachi, the water basin usually of stone material is installed for cleansing of the hands and mouth, and the arrangement of the set of Tsukubai was made with this basin.

Actually, however, the water basin is installed nowadays more for the scenic purpose than for its practical use.

4   手水鉢 (1)

水をたたえる鉢、これは普通、石でつくられているが、この鉢を手水鉢といっている。手や口を清める水の容器というところだ。蹲踞はこれを中心に組んだものであった。

しかし本来の使われ方を離れて、庭の景色のポイントとして据えることも多い。つまり実用でなく鑑賞主体にも扱えるわけだ。

40

71

92

50

51

4 The Chozubachi (2)

While the *Chozubachi* is mostly of stone, it has many styles and forms. Some *Chozubachi* is merely a piece of natural rock on which a hole is cut, called *Mizuana*, to contain water. Other *Chozubachi* may be worked on to square or round shape, even with sculptures on the sides. Some *Chozubachi* is designed in straight lines only.

4 手水鉢 (2)

手水鉢は石を材料とするものがほとんどだが、それらにしても、自然石に水をたたえる穴（水穴という）を彫っただけのものや、角や丸形に加工し、彫刻まで外側に施したようなものまで、その形状はさまざまである。

特に直線のデザインによるものなど清新な感じもして面白い。

26

89

29

91

39

"CHOZU-BACHI" WATER BASIN
(STAND TYPE)

74

14

41

80

81

5 The Waterfall

In Japan the waterfall in the garden is built mostly depicting its form as seen in nature.   Often water is made to drop in two or three stages in order to emphasize the visual effect.   In some case the drop of water is made several meters high.

In recent years the waterfall is built indoors, or even in a narrow court yard due to the advance of artificial stone making.

5　瀧

　庭の中の瀧も、日本の場合は自然の瀧の形を写したものがほとんどである。従って水の落とし方に工夫を凝らすことが多い。二段、三段というように何度も水を落下させて楽しみを倍増したり、一条の水を高くから落としたりと、そのデザインもいたって多様である。

　最近は人造石の発達で室内、中庭にもつくられている。

47

58

61

44

45

6 Izutsu, or the stone well-curb, and Bridges

Izutsu is Japanese term of the former stone curb of the sunken well and used in the garden for its interesting shape either round or square as the source of water.

Bridges in the garden are mainly of stone, either natural or artificially cut, each material giving different effects.   The wooden bridge gives a soft effect, and is used in such place as the pond with water plants.

6 井筒と橋

井筒というのは井戸の上部を囲った設備であって、井戸側とも呼ばれている。これには円形のもの、四角のものなどいろいろあるが、庭では水源の表現をするとき、よく使われる。

庭の橋は石材のものが主体だが、これも自然石、加工石によって味が違う。木の橋は柔らかさが出て水草中心の池などに好まれる。

31

77

85

10

7

7   Kakehi, the Bamboo-piping, and Suisha, the waterwheel

Kakehi is the Japanese term of the water carrying bamboo pipe line above the ground, either of whole or split bamboo.   The spring water from hidden source is carried by *Kakehi* usually pourd to the water bowl in the garden.   Garden view may differ by the length of *Kakehi* line.

Suisha, the waterwheel, of the former motor power of the mill, is still utilized as a garden scene because of its charming form and motion.

7　筧と水車

筧は水を通す設備で、普通は竹を使う。この筧を伝った水が手水鉢に流れ込んでくるわけで、いわば水源にも当たる場合が多い。その長さによって景色自体にも変化が出る。そこで筧中心の庭といったものも考え出されるようになるのだ。

水車は動力の一種だが、庭の景としても結構楽しめる素材である。

94

88

42

43

PLAN／庭の図面

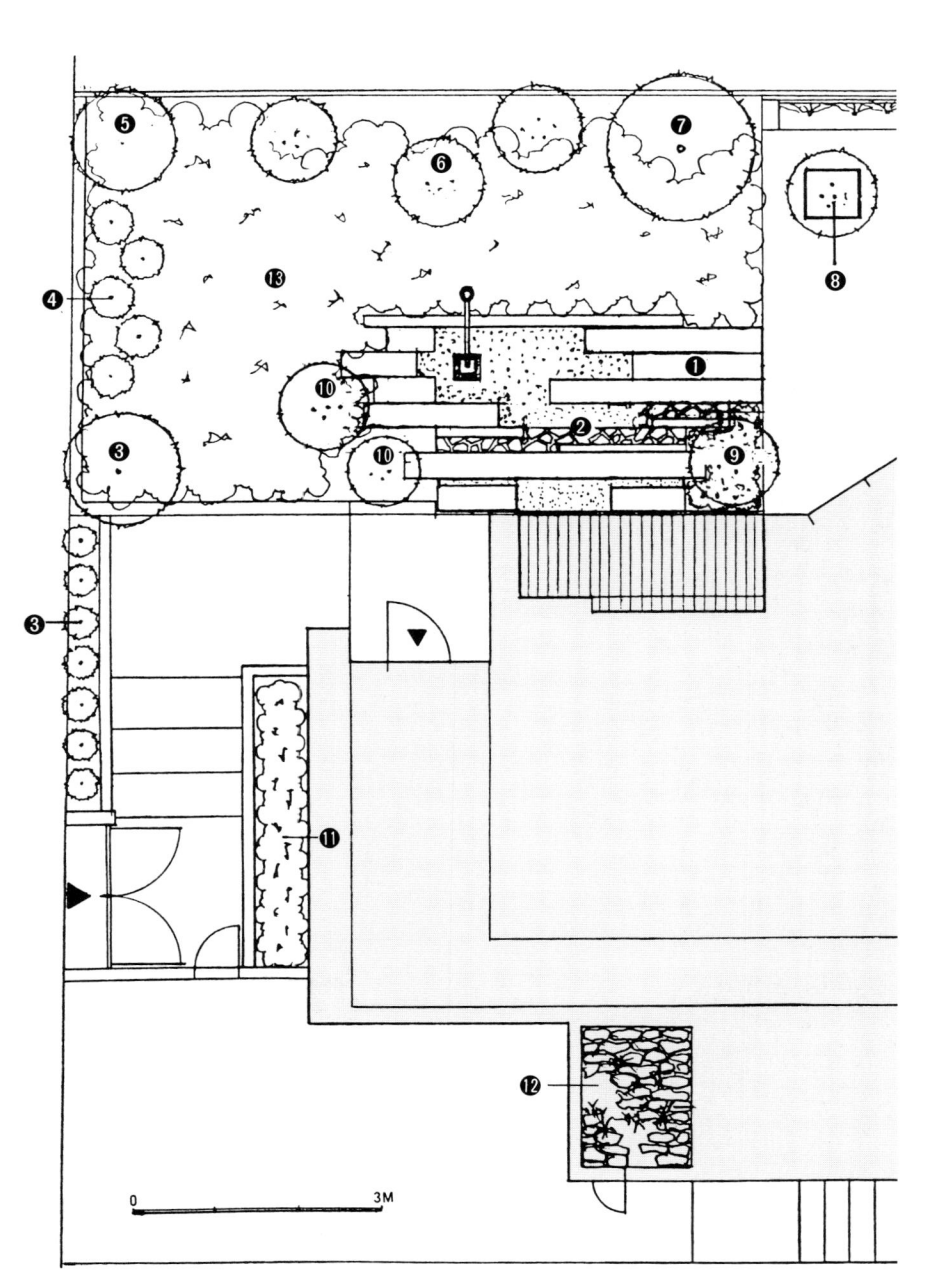

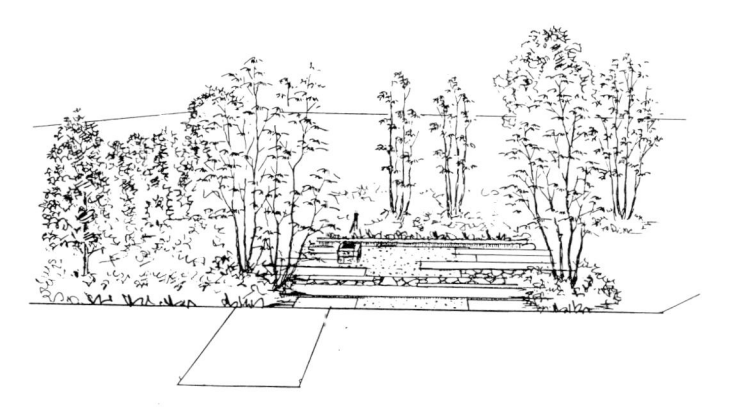

14 Nagoya Estate (Work of Eiichi Kawayauchi)
名古屋邸（川谷内映一作品）

❶	SHIRAKAWAISHI PAVEMENT	白川石敷き
❷	TANBAISHI PAVED NOBEDAN	丹波石貼り延段
❸	TEA-OIL PLANT	サザンカ
❹	COMMON CAMELLIA	タチカンツバキ
❺	FRAGRANT OLIVE	モクセイ
❻	BOUGASHI TREE	ボウガシ
❼	BAYBERRY	ヤマモモ
❽	JAPANESE DOGWOOD	ヤマボウシ
❾	MAPLE-TREE SHRUBBIES	モミジ株立
❿	MAPLE-TREE	モミジ
⓫	JAPANESE MAHONIA	ヒイラギナンテン
⓬	GRAND COVER PLANTS AND DAIMYŌCHIKU BAMBOO IN THE NEBUKAWAISHI STONE TERRACE	根府川石敷きの間に下草及びダイミョウチク
⓭	SATSUKI AZALEA SHRUBBIES	サツキ・ツツジ寄植え

14 Nagoya Estate (Work of Eiichi Kawayauchi)
名古屋邸（川谷内映一作品）

16 Itō Estate (Work of Ken Dōke)
伊藤邸（道家健作品）

❶	DINING ROOM	食 堂
❷	SAKURAGAWA GRAVEL SCRUBBED FINISH	桜川砂利洗出
❸	MOSS	苔
❹	KISOISHI NOBEDAN	木曽石延段
❺	KISOISHI TOBIISHI (PATH)	木曽石飛石
❻	DRAIN MEASURE	排水桝
❼	KISOISHI STONE BRIDGE	石橋（木曽石）
❽	ISLAND	中 島
❾	AJIROGAKI (FENCE)	網代垣
❿	RENJIGAKI (FENCE)	連子垣
⓫	AMIDAGAKI (FENCE)	阿弥陀垣

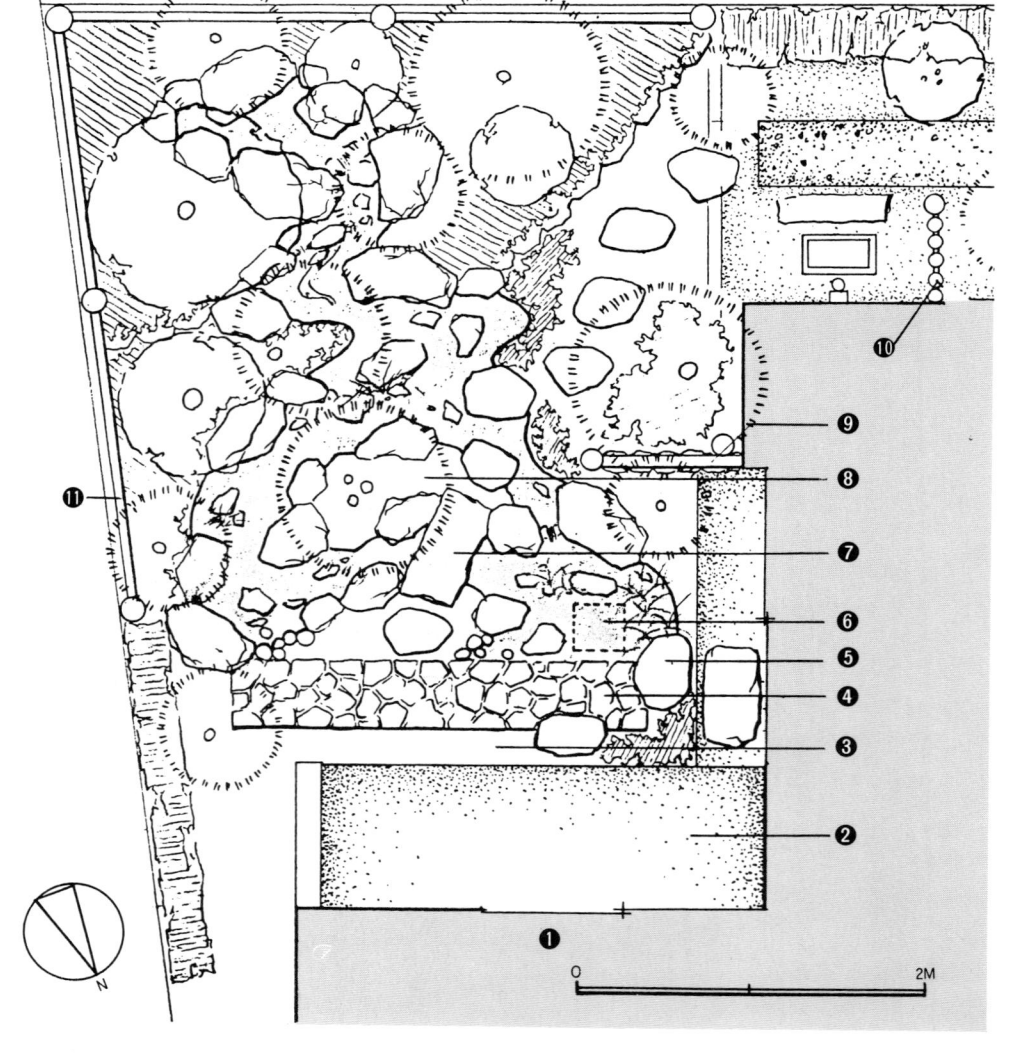

16 Itō Estate (Work of Ken Dōke)
伊藤邸（道家健作品）

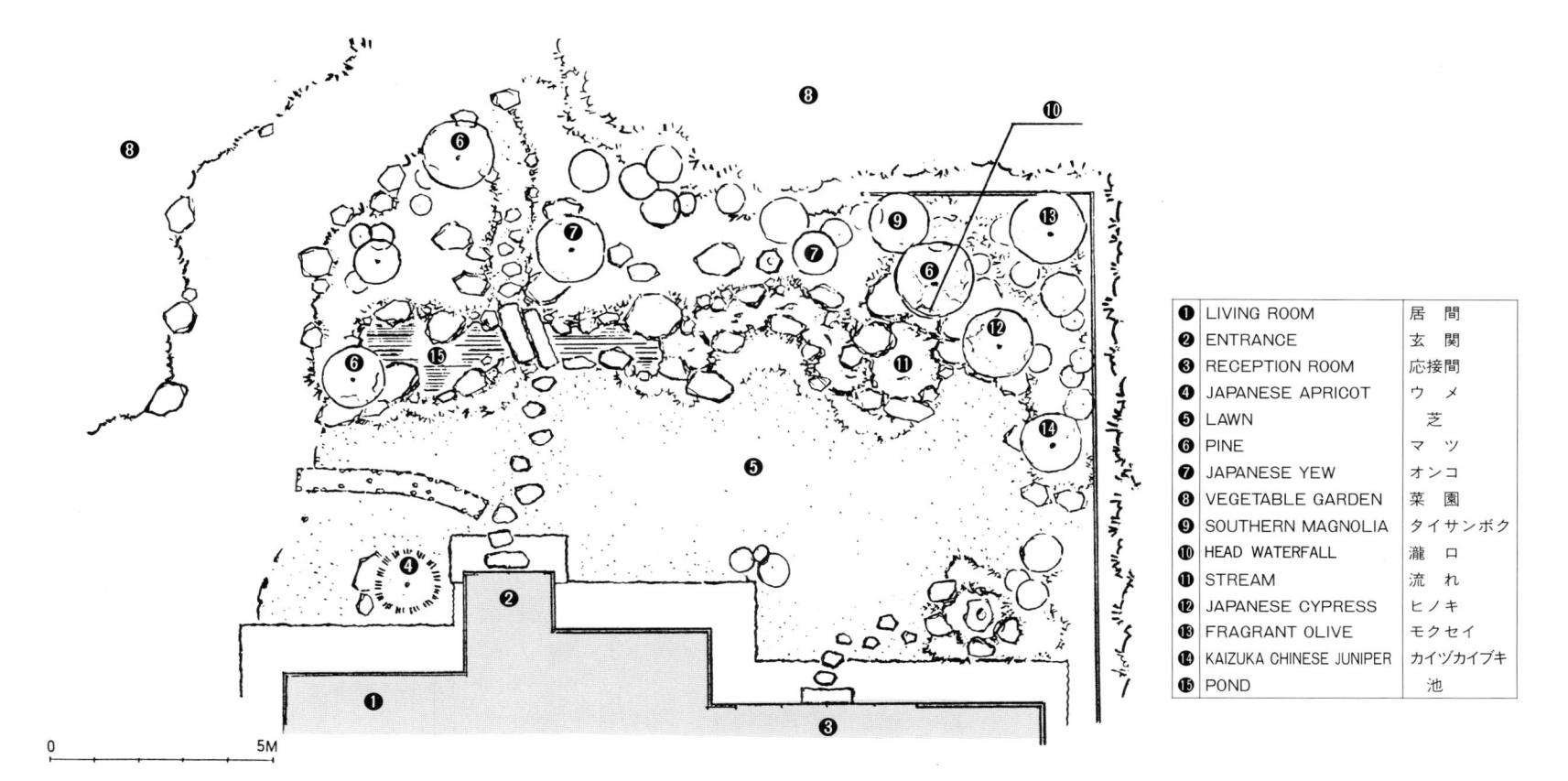

❶	LIVING ROOM	居 間
❷	ENTRANCE	玄 関
❸	RECEPTION ROOM	応接間
❹	JAPANESE APRICOT	ウ メ
❺	LAWN	芝
❻	PINE	マ ツ
❼	JAPANESE YEW	オンコ
❽	VEGETABLE GARDEN	菜 園
❾	SOUTHERN MAGNOLIA	タイサンボク
❿	HEAD WATERFALL	瀧 口
⓫	STREAM	流 れ
⓬	JAPANESE CYPRESS	ヒノキ
⓭	FRAGRANT OLIVE	モクセイ
⓮	KAIZUKA CHINESE JUNIPER	カイヅカイブキ
⓯	POND	池

5 Ōba Estate (Work of Asaji Moroi)
大場邸（諸井浅次作品）

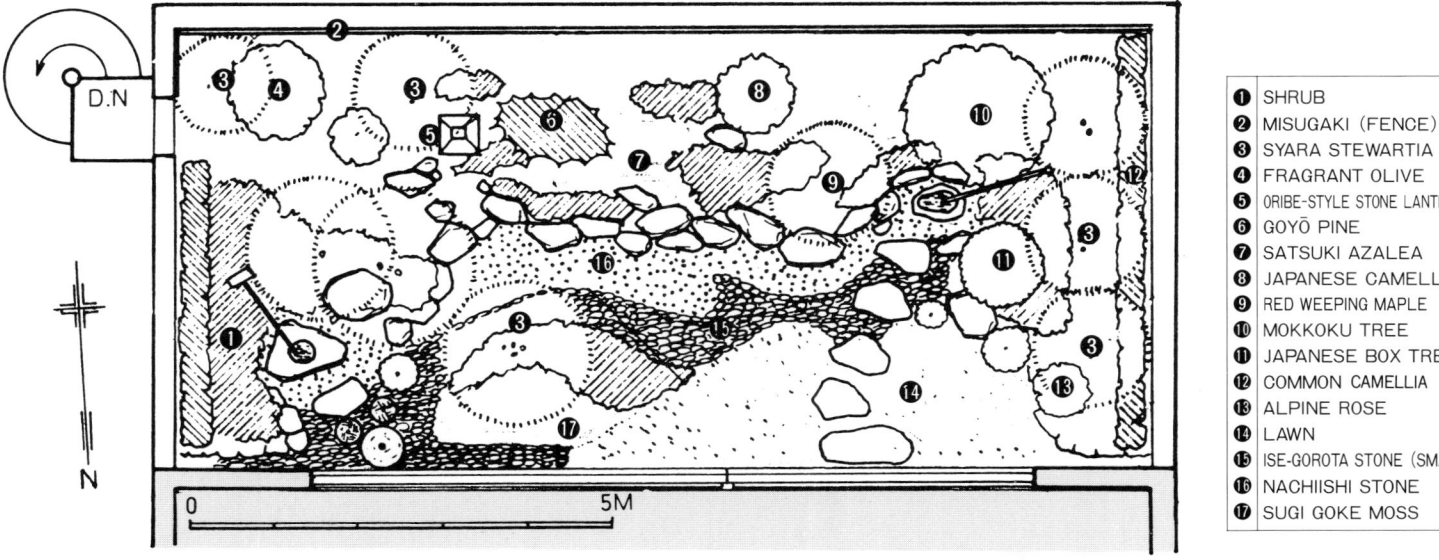

❶	SHRUB	灌 木
❷	MISUGAKI (FENCE)	御簾垣
❸	SYARA STEWARTIA	シャラ
❹	FRAGRANT OLIVE	モクセイ
❺	ORIBE-STYLE STONE LANTERN	織部形石燈籠
❻	GOYŌ PINE	ゴヨウマツ
❼	SATSUKI AZALEA	サツキ
❽	JAPANESE CAMELLIA	ヤブツバキ
❾	RED WEEPING MAPLE	ベニシダレモミジ
❿	MOKKOKU TREE	モッコク
⓫	JAPANESE BOX TREE	ツ ゲ
⓬	COMMON CAMELLIA	カンツバキ
⓭	ALPINE ROSE	シャクナゲ
⓮	LAWN	芝
⓯	ISE-GOROTA STONE (SMALL)	伊勢ゴロタ
⓰	NACHIISHI STONE	那智石
⓱	SUGI GOKE MOSS	スギゴケ

21 Shiga Estate (Work of Chiaki Kobayashi)
志賀邸（小林千秋作品）

22·23 Kashima Estate (Work of Eiichi Kawayauchi)
鹿島邸(川谷内映一作品)

26 Meikō Shōkai (Work of Ken Dōke)
明光商会(道家健作品)

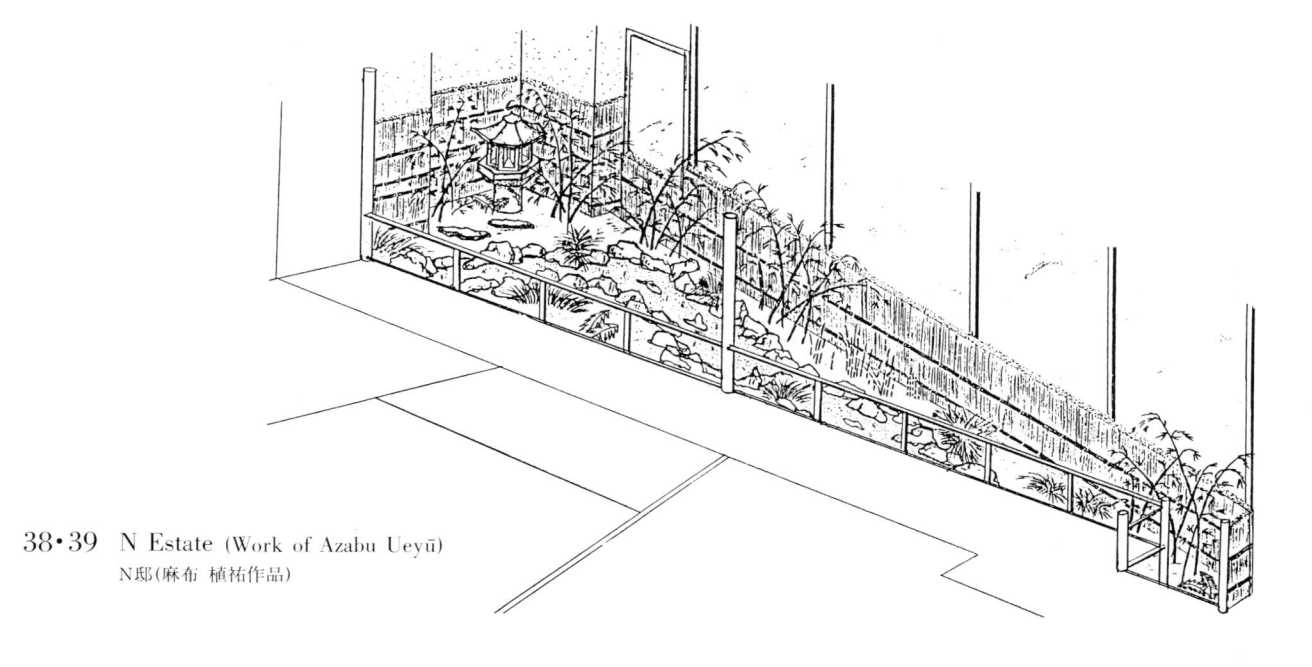

38・39 N Estate (Work of Azabu Ueyū)
N邸（麻布 植祐作品）

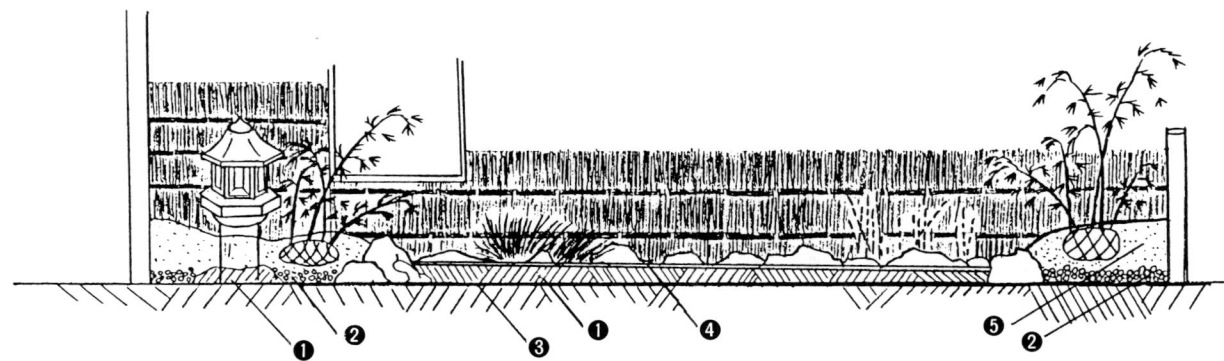

❶	MORTAR	モルタル
❷	DRAINING STRATUM	排水層
❸	MORTAR WATERPROOF	防水モルタル
❹	ŌISO GRAVEL SCRUBBED FINISH	大磯砂利洗出
❺	IMPROVED SOIL	人工改良土壌

38・39 N Estate (Work of Azabu Ueyū)
N邸（麻布 植祐作品）

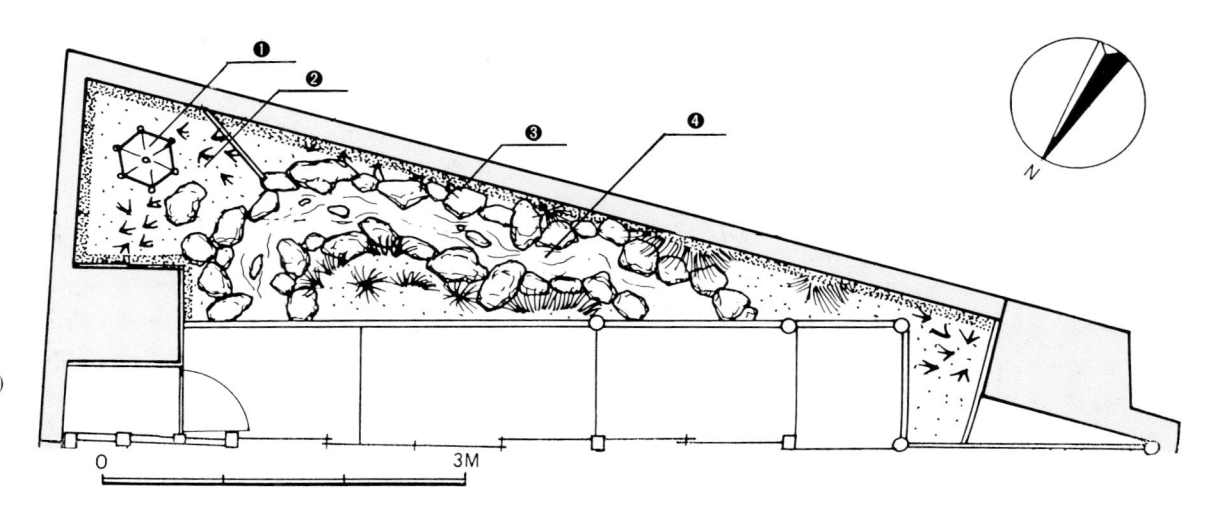

❶	DŌMYŌJI-STYLE STONE LANTERN	導明寺形石燈籠
❷	KANCHIKU BAMBOO	カンチク
❸	KUROMOJIGAKI (FENCE)	クロモジ垣
❹	STREAM	流れ

38・39 N Estate (Work of Azabu Ueyū)
N邸（麻布 植祐作品）

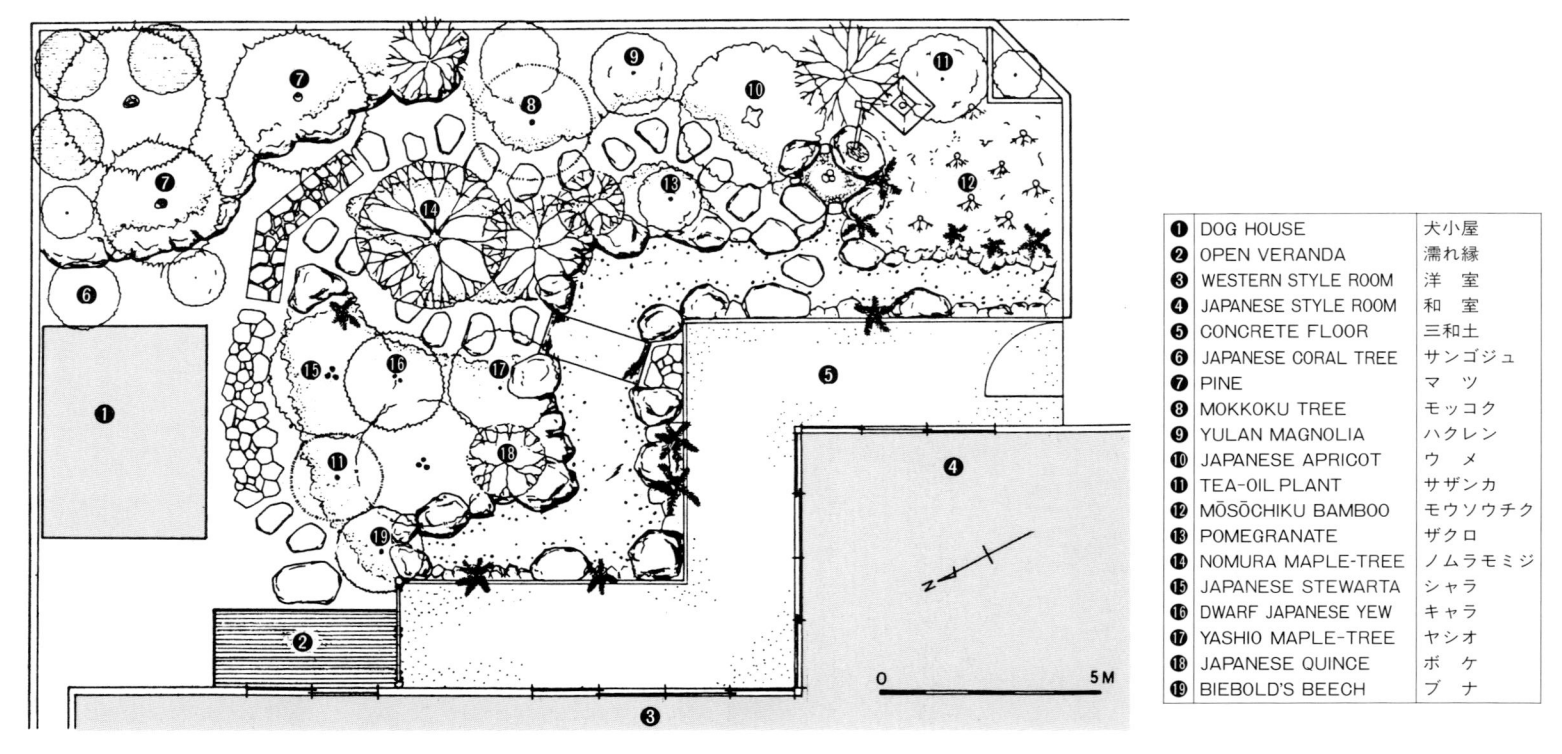

❶	DOG HOUSE	犬小屋
❷	OPEN VERANDA	濡れ縁
❸	WESTERN STYLE ROOM	洋　室
❹	JAPANESE STYLE ROOM	和　室
❺	CONCRETE FLOOR	三和土
❻	JAPANESE CORAL TREE	サンゴジュ
❼	PINE	マ　ツ
❽	MOKKOKU TREE	モッコク
❾	YULAN MAGNOLIA	ハクレン
❿	JAPANESE APRICOT	ウ　メ
⓫	TEA-OIL PLANT	サザンカ
⓬	MŌSŌCHIKU BAMBOO	モウソウチク
⓭	POMEGRANATE	ザクロ
⓮	NOMURA MAPLE-TREE	ノムラモミジ
⓯	JAPANESE STEWARTA	シャラ
⓰	DWARF JAPANESE YEW	キャラ
⓱	YASHIO MAPLE-TREE	ヤシオ
⓲	JAPANESE QUINCE	ボ　ケ
⓳	BIEBOLD'S BEECH	ブ　ナ

57　Tsuruoka Estate (Work of Sōichirō Kinoshita)
　　鶴岡邸（木下荘一郎作品）

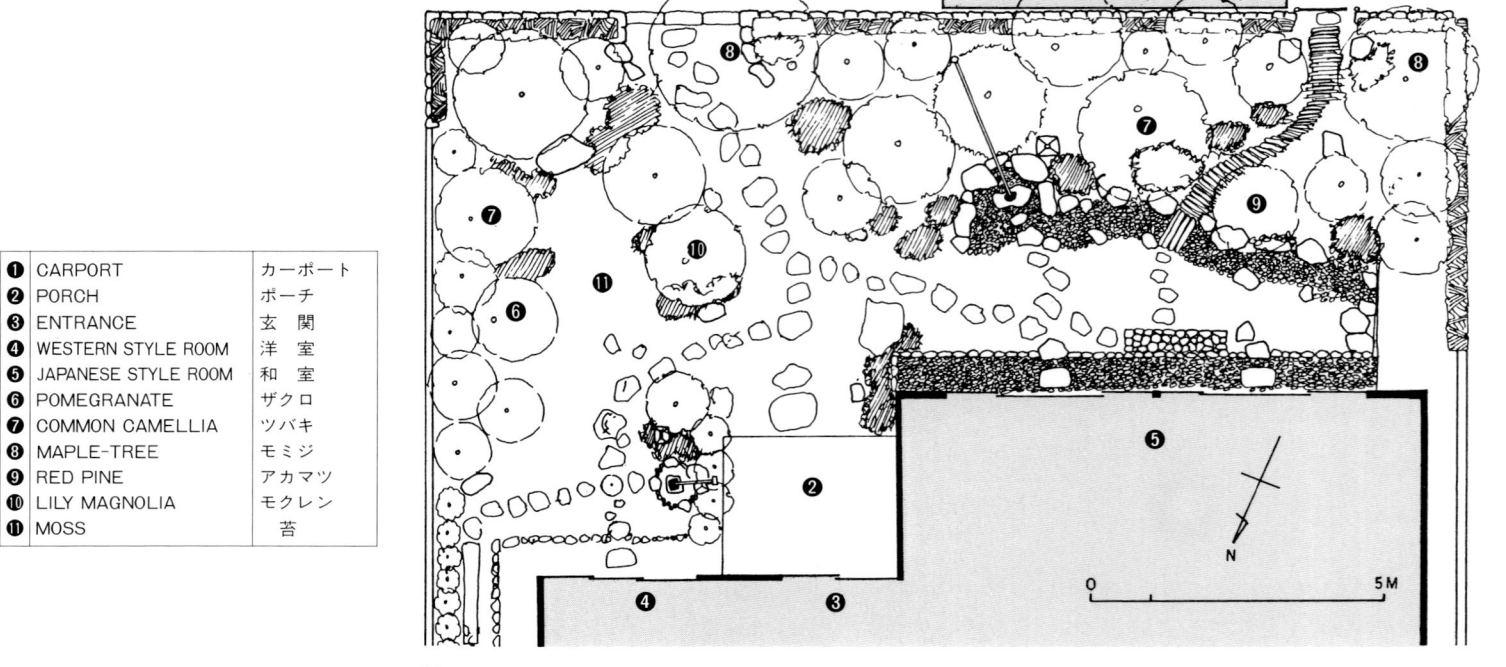

❶	CARPORT	カーポート
❷	PORCH	ポーチ
❸	ENTRANCE	玄関
❹	WESTERN STYLE ROOM	洋　室
❺	JAPANESE STYLE ROOM	和　室
❻	POMEGRANATE	ザクロ
❼	COMMON CAMELLIA	ツバキ
❽	MAPLE-TREE	モミジ
❾	RED PINE	アカマツ
❿	LILY MAGNOLIA	モクレン
⓫	MOSS	苔

65　Ibe Estate (Work of Matsutarō Kanda)
　　井部邸（神田松太郎作品）

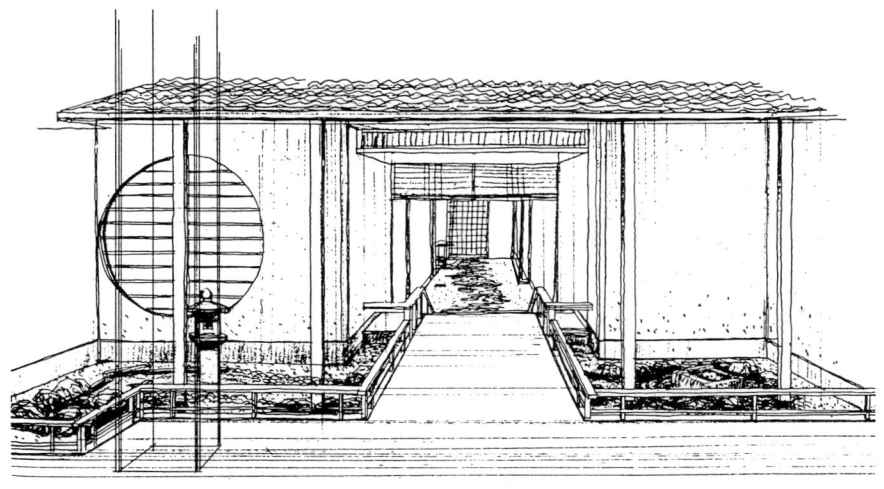

77 Hanamurasaki (Work of Kōzō Iwatani)
花紫（岩谷浩三作品）

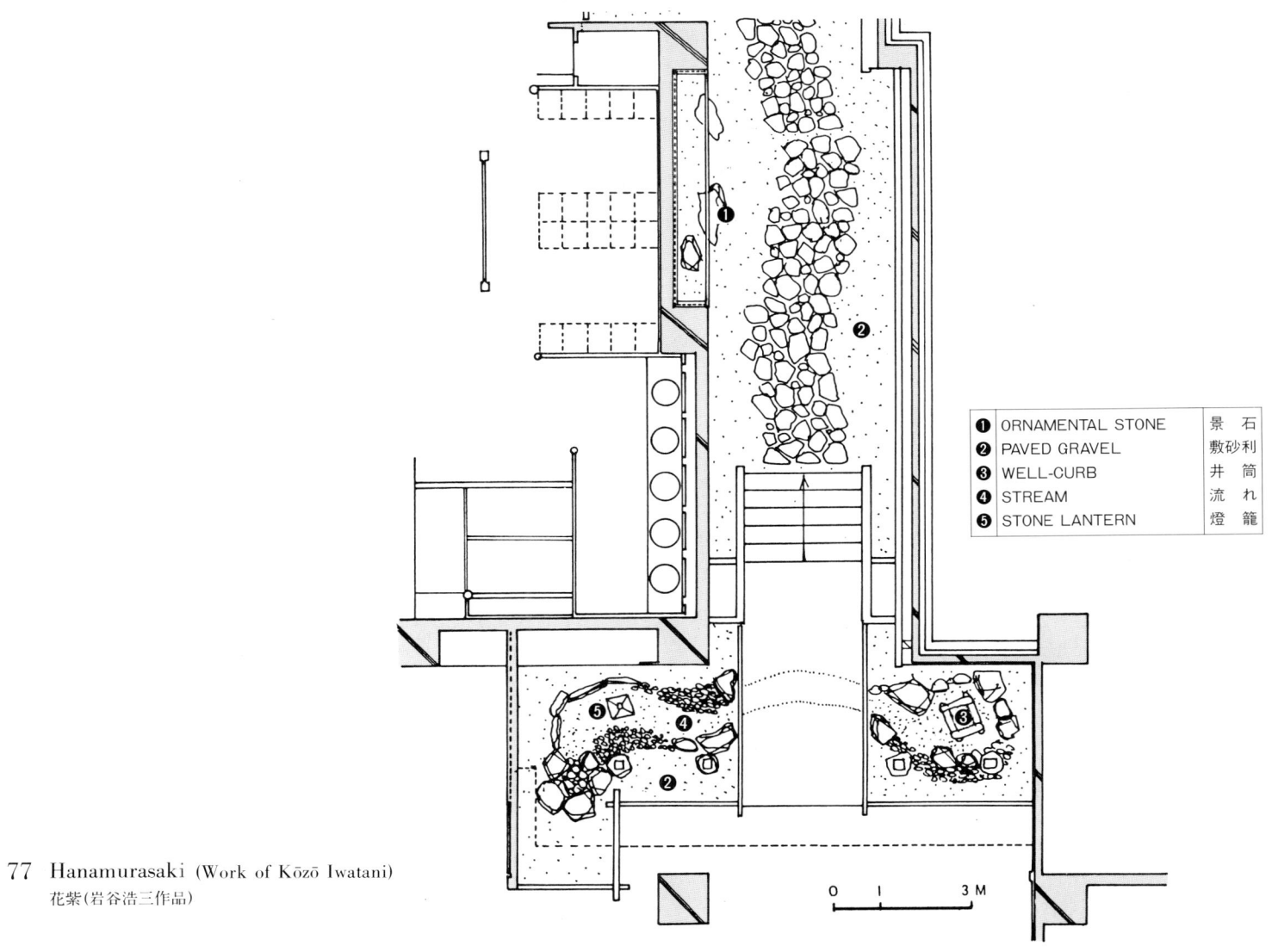

❶	ORNAMENTAL STONE	景　石
❷	PAVED GRAVEL	敷砂利
❸	WELL-CURB	井　筒
❹	STREAM	流　れ
❺	STONE LANTERN	燈　籠

77 Hanamurasaki (Work of Kōzō Iwatani)
花紫（岩谷浩三作品）

L I S T [GARDEN DESIGNER]

NAME (氏名)	ADDRESS (住所)	PHOTO NUMBER (掲載写真番号)
KYŌICHI CHIBA 千葉 恭一	4-21 Sanbongi, Mizusawa-shi, Iwate Pref. 〒023 0197-24-7801 水沢市三本木4-21 〒023 ☎0197-24-7801	1, 2
HIROSHI MONIWA 茂庭 弘	55 Aza Ochiai, Odaki, Esashi-shi, Iwate Pref. 〒023-11 ☎0197-35-5529 江刺市愛宕字落合55 〒023-11 ☎0197-35-5529	3, 4
ASAJI MOROI 諸井 浅次	1-15 Sakae-chō, Haramachi-shi, Fukushima Pref. 〒975 ☎0244-22-8766 原町市栄町1-15 〒975 ☎0244-22-8766	5
MICHIO MOROI 諸井 道雄	1-112 Ōmachi, Haramachi-shi, Fukushima Pref. 〒975 ☎0244-24-1633 原町市大町1-112 〒975 ☎0244-24-1633	6
KŌJI IKEDA 池田 幸司	537-5 Yokoyama-chō, Utsunomiya-shi, Tochigi Pref. 〒320 ☎0286-24-4094 宇都宮市横山町537-5 〒320 ☎0286-24-4094	7, 8
TOSHIKI TAKAMATSU 高松 俊樹	2179 Yamamoto, Mashiko-machi, Haga-gun, Tochigi Pref. 〒321-42 ☎0285-72-4107 栃木県芳賀郡益子町山本2179 〒321-42 ☎0285-72-4107	9, 10
KŌJI MATSUMOTO 松本 孔志	452 Ōaza-Angyōjirin, Kawaguchi-shi, Saitama Pref. 〒334 ☎0482-95-1231 川口市大字安行慈林452 〒334 ☎0482-95-1231	11
SEIGAKU NAKAMURA 中村 青岳	3-25-4 Shibakubo-chō, Tanashi-shi, Tokyo 〒188 ☎0424-61-5600 田無市芝久保町3-25-4 〒188 ☎0424-61-5600	12, 13
EIICHI KAWAYAUCHI 川谷内 映一	6-5-10 Himonya, Meguro-ku, Tokyo 〒152 ☎03-3710-1258 目黒区碑文谷6-5-10 〒152 ☎03-3710-1258	14, 15, 22, 23
KEN DŌKE 道家 健	5-18-4 Jindaiji-Minami-chō, Chōfu-shi, Tokyo 〒182 ☎0424-83-9669 調布市深大寺南町5-18-4 〒182 ☎0424-83-9669	16, 17, 19, 26 COVER
TOSHIYUKI IWASAWA 岩沢 俊之	3-23-20 Tsukushino, Machida-shi, Tokyo 〒194 ☎0427-96-1177 町田市つくし野3-23-20 〒194 ☎0427-96-1177	18, 24, 25, 56
SOZAN KAWAMURA 河村 素山	1-7-51 Kitano, Mitaka-shi, Tokyo 〒181 ☎0422-43-2204 三鷹市北野1-7-51 〒182 ☎0422-43-2204	20, 28
CHIAKI KOBAYASHI 小林 千秋	39 Ōaza Kyūzaemonshinden, Kawaguchi-shi, Saitama Pref. 〒333 ☎0482-92-1023 川口市大字久佐ヱ門新田39 〒333 ☎0482-92-1023	21, 31
TAKEYUKI ITAKURA 板倉 武幸	2-1-1 Kamiishihara, Chōfu-shi, Tokyo 〒182 ☎0424-85-7195 調布市上石原2-1-1 〒182 ☎0424-85-7195	27
MIKI FUJINO 藤野 三樹	4-9-10 Nishiikuta, Tama-ku, Kawasaki-shi, Kanagawa Pref. 〒214 ☎044-966-3819 川崎市多摩区西生田4-9-10 〒214 ☎044-966-3819	29
TOSHIO HASHIMOTO 橋本 年男	3-22-10 Igusa, Suginami-ku, Tokyo 〒167 ☎03-3390-1826 杉並区井草3-22-10 〒167 ☎03-3390-1826	30, 48
TAKAYUKI HIRAI 平井 孝幸	3-7-2 Shinmachi, Hōya-shi, Tokyo 〒202 ☎0422-52-1058 保谷市新町3-7-2 〒202 ☎0422-52-1058	32
TŌKAI ZŌEN 東海造園	4-17-7 Minami-Shinagawa, Shinagawa-ku, Tokyo 〒140 ☎03-3474-5303 品川区南品川4-17-7 〒140 ☎03-3474-5303	33, 35
YAMAMOTO ZŌEN 山本造園	7-6-50 Akasaka, Minato-ku, Tokyo 〒107 ☎03-3585-2341 港区赤坂7-6-50 〒107 ☎03-3585-2341	34
MITSUKOSHI GREEN CENTER-BU 三越グリーンセンター部	1-4-1 Muromachi, Nihonbashi, Chūō-ku, Tokyo 〒103 ☎03-3241-3311 中央区日本橋室町1-4-1 〒103 ☎03-3241-3311	36, 37
AZABU UEYŪ 麻布 植祐	3-3-31 Minami-Azabu, Minato-ku, Tokyo 〒106 ☎03-3444-3995 港区南麻布3-3-31 〒106 ☎03-3444-3995	38, 39, 41
HAYAMA ZŌEN 羽山造園	1-20-8 Nagasaki, Toshima-ku, Tokyo 〒171 ☎03-3974-1682 豊島区長崎1-20-8 〒171 ☎03-3974-1682	40
TŌKAI NŌEN 東海農園	1-25-14 Shimotakaido, Suginami-ku, Tokyo 〒168 ☎03-3302-1545 杉並区下高井戸1-25-14 〒168 ☎03-3302-1545	42, 43
SEIWA ZŌEN 成和造園	6-7-17 Matsubara, Setagaya-ku, Tokyo 〒156 ☎03-3328-1315 世田谷区松原6-7-17 〒156 ☎03-3328-1315	44
SEIJI IMANAKA 今中 征治	3-9-14 Oyamadai, Setagaya-ku, Tokyo 〒158 ☎03-3704-6835 世田谷区尾山台3-9-14 〒158 ☎03-3704-6835	45
TOMIO INOUE 井上 富雄	971 Aoyama, Tsukui-machi, Tsukui-gun, Kanagawa Pref. 〒220-02 ☎0427-84-4854 神奈川県津久井郡津久井町青山971 〒220-02 ☎0427-84-4854	46, 47, 54, 55
MIKIO TOMITA 富田 幹雄	783-3 Miyazawa-chō, Seya-ku, Yokohama-shi, Kanagawa Pref. 〒246 ☎045-301-5168 横浜市瀬谷区宮沢町783-3 〒246 ☎045-301-5168	49

NAME (氏名)	ADDRESS (住所)	PHOTO NUMBER (掲載写真番号)
HIROSHI NAKAMURA 中村　寛	1-8-11 Tamazutsumi, Setagaya-ku, Tokyo　〒158　☎03-3704-1097 世田谷区玉堤1-8-11　〒158　☎03-3704-1097	50, 51
MASAYUKI KOJIMA 小嶋　正行	505 Shimo-kuzawa, Sagamihara-shi, Kanagawa Pref.　〒229　☎0427-62-2666 相模原市下九沢505　〒229　☎0427-62-2666	52, 53
SŌICHIRŌ KINOSHITA 木下　荘一郎	5-4-17 Shin-Nakahama, Niigata-shi, Niigata Pref.　〒950-21　☎0252-62-0961 新潟市新中浜5-4-17　〒950-21　☎0252-62-0961	57
IKECHŪ ZŌEN 池忠　造園	3-16 Takara-chō, Kashiwazaki-shi, Niigata Pref.　〒945　☎0257-22-6532 柏崎市宝町3-16　〒945　☎0257-22-6532	58, 59
TAKAO DONUMA 土沼　隆雄	37 Ōshima, Niigata-shi, Niigata Pref.　〒950　☎025-285-5088 新潟市大島37　〒950　☎025-285-5088	60
WAKASUGI ZŌEN 若杉　造園	12-ku Maki-chō, Nishikanbara-gun, Niigata Pref.　〒953　☎02567-2-3080 新潟県西蒲原郡巻町12区　〒953　☎02567-2-3080	61
TAKEUCHI ZŌEN 竹内　造園	1-3-4 Shinei-chō, Shibata-shi, Niigata Pref.　〒957　☎0254-22-3973 新発田市新栄町1-3-4　〒957　☎0254-22-3973	62, 63, 64
MATSUTARŌ KANDA 神田　松太郎	2441 Ōaza Shirone, Shirone-shi, Niigata Pref.　〒950-12　☎025-372-2605 白根市大字白根2441　〒950-12　☎025-372-2605	65
SHŌZŌ ISHIKAWA 石川　昇造	9-42 Mizushima-chō, Niigata-shi, Niigata Pref.　〒950　☎025-244-0998 新潟市水島町9-42　〒950　☎025-244-0998	66
HOKURIKU ZŌEN 北陸　造園	15-21 Terao-asahidōri, Niigata-shi, Niigata Pref.　〒950　☎025-266-9430 新潟市寺尾朝日通15-21　〒950　☎025-266-9430	67, 68
KATSUYOSHI KISHI 城至　勝義	Ka-256 Hasadani-machi, Komatsu-shi, Ishikawa Pref.　〒923-01　☎0761-46-1101 小松市波佐谷町カ256　〒923-01　☎0761-46-1101	69
TOMIO TAKEBAYASHI 竹林　臣夫	73 Saiku-chō, Komatsu-shi, Ishikawa Pref.　〒923　☎0761-22-2027 小松市細工町73　〒923　☎0761-22-2027	70
TAKESHI TACHIBANA 立花　武志	Ta-105 Terai, Terai-chō, Nomi-gun, Ishikawa Pref.　〒923-11　☎07615-7-4128 石川県能美郡寺井町寺井た105　〒923-11　☎07615-7-4128	71, 72
SHIGEJI TAKEBAYASHI 竹林　繁二	73 Saiku-chō, Komatsu-shi, Ishikawa Pref.　〒923　☎0761-22-2027 小松市細工町73　〒923　☎0761-22-2027	73, 74
TOMIGO ICHIMURA 市村　冨五	Nu-43 Hirugawa-machi, Komatsu-shi, Ishikawa Pref.　〒923　☎0761-22-5601 小松市蛭川町ヌ43　〒923　☎0761-22-5601	75
SEIKICHI MATSUMOTO 松本　清吉	1-29-1 Higashiyama, Kanazawa-shi, Ishikawa Pref.　〒920　☎0762-52-6788 金沢市東山1-29-1　〒920　☎0762-52-6788	76
KŌZŌ IWATANI 岩谷　浩三	2-129 Nishikarumi-machi, Komatsu-shi, Ishikawa Pref.　〒923　☎0761-47-2841 小松市西軽海町2-129　〒923　☎0761-47-2841	77, 78, 79
SABURŌ SONE 曽根　三郎	255-6 Haradaniinui-chō, Ōkitayama, Kita-ku, Kyoto-shi, Kyoto Pref.　〒603　☎075-462-6058 京都市北区大北山原谷乾町255-6　〒603　☎075-462-6058	80, 81
TAKAHIRO INOUE 井上　剛宏	11 Nishihachigaoka, Uzumasa, Ukyō-ku, Kyoto-shi, Kyoto Pref.　〒616　☎075-861-2880 京都市右京区太秦西蜂ヶ岡11　〒616　☎075-861-2880	82, 83
KŌZŌ OKAMOTO 岡本　耕蔵	1-9 Idegakaidō-chō, Matsugasaki, Sakyō-ku, Kyoto-shi, Kyoto Pref.　〒606　☎075-791-2522 京都市左京区松ヶ崎井出ヶ海道町1-9　〒606　☎075-791-2522	84
SHŌJI INOHANA 猪鼻　昌司	4-31 Hinookanishi-chō, Fushimi-ku, Kyoto-shi, Kyoto Pref.　〒601-13　☎075-572-1546 京都市伏見区日野岡西町4-31　〒601-13　☎075-572-1546	85, 86, 93, 94
MINORU FUJII 藤井　稔	11-24 Ishidaōyama-chō, Fushimi-ku, Kyoto-shi, Kyoto Pref.　〒601-13　☎075-571-3685 京都市伏見区石田大山町11-24　〒601-13　☎075-571-3685	87
HIDEO TSUDA 津田　秀夫	37 Shimoōji-chō, Yoshida, Sakyō-ku, Kyoto-shi, Kyoto Pref.　〒606　☎075-771-4928 京都市左京区吉田下大路町37　〒606　☎075-771-4928	88, 89
YASUO KITAYAMA 北山　安夫	1-11 Naka-machi, Tōjiin, Kita-ku, Kyoto-shi, Kyoto Pref.　〒603　☎075-463-4945 京都市北区等持院中町1-11　〒603　☎075-463-4945	90
MASAFUMI KOBAYASHI 小林　正典	1138 Hataeda-chō, Iwakura, Sakyō-ku, Kyoto-shi, Kyoto Pref.　〒606　☎075-791-8167 京都市左京区岩倉幡枝町1138　〒606　☎075-791-8167	91
YUKIO TERASAKI 寺崎　幸雄	4-16 Hinogami-chō, Matsugasaki, Sakyō-ku, Kyoto-shi, Kyoto Pref.　〒606　☎075-722-6251 京都市左京区松ヶ崎樋ノ上町4-16　〒606　☎075-722-6251	92

MAP (DISTRIBUTION)

No.	PREFECTURE(都道府県)	PHOTO NUMBER(写真番号)
❶	IWATE(岩手)	1, 2, 3, 4
❷	FUKUSHIMA(福島)	5, 6
❸	TOCHIGI(栃木)	7, 8, 9, 10
❹	SAITAMA(埼玉)	11, 12, 13
❺	TOKYO(東京)	14, 15, 16, 17, 18, 19, 20, 21, 22, 23, 24, 25, 26, 27, 28, 29, 30, 31, 32, 33, 34, 35, 36, 37, 38, 39, 40, 41, 42, 43, 44, 45, COVER
❻	KANAGAWA(神奈川)	46, 47, 48, 49, 50, 51, 52, 53, 54, 55, 56
❼	NIIGATA(新潟)	57, 58, 59, 60, 61, 62, 63, 64, 65, 66, 67, 68
❽	ISHIKAWA(石川)	69, 70, 71, 72, 73, 74, 75, 76, 77, 78, 79
❾	KYOTO(京都)	80, 81, 82, 83, 84, 85, 86, 87, 88, 89, 90, 91, 92
❿	NARA(奈良)	93, 94

AFTERWORD

The aim of this series of publications is to introduce far and wide by whom and under what kind of designs the present day Japanese gardens are being planned and constructed.

The present series No. 3 introduces specifically those gardens where the handling of water and its manner of flowing is the main concern. It is hoped that the readers will realize the fact that handling of water is just as varied as handling of stones in the Japanese garedn.

In this series No.3, as in other series, the works introduced are not confined to the limited numbers of the up-coming artists' works but many of the local veteran's works are presented, making the volume rich in variety. You will find how the Japanese gardens of water are being activated at present.

あ と が き

このシリーズは、現代の日本の庭は、どんな人たちによって、どんなデザインのもとにつくられているかを、ひろく紹介することを目的としています。

第3巻は特に水と流れの庭にスポットを当ててみました。日本の庭の特色の一つに、水の扱い方も石の扱い方と同様に多彩であることを知っていただくためです。

第3巻でも新鋭だけでなく、各地のベテランの作品も加えてバラエティーに富んだものとしています。

日本的な水の庭が、現代にどう生かされているかご覧下さい。

庭 GARDEN VIEWS III
—WATER & STREAM GARDENS—

First Edition January 1991

Planner & Editor : Takenosuke Tatsui (Tatsui Teien Kenkyujo)
Fukuda Bldg. 1-6-3 Nishi-waseda,
Shinjuku-ku, Tokyo 169
Tel.03-3202-5233 Fax.03-3202-5394
Publisher : Eihachirō Baba
Published : Kenchiku Shiryō Kenkyusha, Ltd.
Tokyū Nishi No.3 Bldg. 1-15-7 Nishi-ikebukuro,
Toshima-ku, Tokyo 171
Tel.03-3986-3239 Fax.03-3987-3256
Printed : Toppan Printing Co., Ltd.

All rights reserved. No part of this book may be produced or used in any form or by any means without written permission from the publisher. A reviewer may quote brief passages.

ISBN4-87460-250-9

庭 GARDEN VIEWS III
—水と流れの庭—

1991年1月15日 初版発行

企画・編著者：龍居竹之介（龍居庭園研究所）
東京都新宿区西早稲田1-6-3 福田ビル3F 〒169
Tel.03-3202-5233 Fax.03-3202-5394
発　行　者：馬場瑛八郎
発　行　所：株式会社 建築資料研究社
東京都豊島区西池袋1-15-7 藤久西3号館8F 〒171
Tel.03-3986-3239 Fax.03-3987-3256
印　刷　所：凸版印刷株式会社

〈禁無断複製〉　　ISBN4-87460-250-9